GARLANDS FOR CHRISTMAS

Garlands

FOR

CHRISTMAS

A SELECTION OF POETRY

EDITED, WITH AN INTRODUCTION, BY

Chad Walsh

THE MACMILLAN COMPANY
NEW YORK

ACKNOWLEDGMENTS

THE BODLEY HEAD LTD. Roy Campbell, "Nativity," from *Collected Poems*, Vol. II.

JONATHAN CAPE LIMITED. W. H. Davies, "Christmas," from *Collected Poems*. By permission of the publisher and Mrs. H. M. Davies.

THE CHRISTIAN CENTURY. Jeremy Ingalls, "First Came Christmas," copyright 1964, Christian Century Foundation. Reprinted by permission from the December 13, 1964 issue of *The Christian Century*.

DODD, MEAD & COMPANY. "A Christmas Carol" from *The Collected Poems of G. K. Chesterton*. Reprinted by permission of Dodd, Mead & Company from *The Collected Poems of G. K. Chesterton*. Copyright, 1932, by Dodd, Mead & Company, Inc.

ROBERT HALE LTD. Peter Champkin, "The Invoice Clerk," from *The Enmity of Noon*.

HARCOURT, BRACE & WORLD, INC. "Christmas in Black Rock," from *Lord Weary's Castle*, copyright, 1944, 1946, by Robert Lowell. Reprinted by permission of Harcourt, Brace & World, Inc.

HOLT, RINEHART AND WINSTON, INC. Untitled poem, from *In the Clearing* by Robert Frost. Copyright © 1956, 1962 by Robert Frost. Reprinted by permission of Holt, Rinehart and Winston, Inc.

JEREMY INGALLS. "First Came Christmas."

SY KAHN. "Annunciation."

THE MACMILLAN COMPANY (New York). Daniel Berrigan, "Magi." Reprinted with permission of The Macmillan Company from *Time Without Number* by Daniel Berrigan. Copyright 1952 and 1957 by Daniel Berrigan. Edwin Arlington Robinson, "Karma." Reprinted with permission of The Macmillan Company from *Collected Poems* by Edward Arlington Robinson. Copyright 1925 by The Macmillan Company, renewed 1952 by Ruth Nivison and Barbara R. Holt. William Butler Yeats, "The Mother of God." Reprinted with permission of The Macmillan Company from *Collected Poems*

THE UNIVERSITY OF NORTH CAROLINA PRESS. Arnold Kenseth, "An Adoration," "Dürer's Nativity," "A Cycle of Praise," from *The Holy Merriment*.

THE VIKING PRESS, INC. "The Ballad of Befana." From *Merry Christmas, Happy New Year* by Phyllis McGinley. Copyright © 1957 by Phyllis McGinley. Reprinted by permission of The Viking Press, Inc. "Ecce Puer" from *Collected Poems* by James Joyce. Copyright 1918 by B. W. Heubsch, Inc., 1946 by Nora Joyce. Reprinted by permission of The Viking Press, Inc.

CHAD WALSH. "Christmas in the Straw," from *Eden Two-Way*, copyright 1954 by Chad Walsh.

WESLEYAN UNIVERSITY PRESS. Vassar Miller, "Christmas Mourning." Reprinted by permission from *Wage War on Silence*, published 1960 by Wesleyan University Press.

The poems by Southwell are from the Doubleday Anchor edition of *The Meditative Poem: An Anthology of Seventeenth-Century Verse*, edited by Louis L. Martz. Copyright © 1963 by Louis L. Martz.

The poems by Wither and Dunbar are taken from *The Oxford Book of Seventeenth Century Verse* and *The Oxford Book of Christian Verse* respectively.

I am indebted to many persons who suggested particular poems for this book. One in particular I should like to single out by name, for special acknowledgment. Prof. Steve J. Van Der Weele shared with me the extensive research he has done in modern religious verse, and greatly aided me by his generosity.

FOR ED AND CAROL DELL

—AND YOUNG CHAD, HEATHER, AND SARA—

this Christmas token of love

Contents

Introduction

The first Christmas poem was composed by the "armies of heaven," as J. B. Phillips renders the familiar "heavenly host" of the King James Bible. St. Luke sets the scene. First, there are the shepherds out in the open fields. Suddenly they are confronted by a gleaming angel with a message: "Fear not: for, behold, I bring you good tidings of great joy, which shall be to all people. For unto you is born this day in the city of David a Saviour, which is Christ the Lord. And this shall be a sign unto you; Ye shall find the babe wrapped in swaddling clothes, lying in a manger." Barely has the angel finished speaking to the startled shepherds when he is suddenly joined by "a multitude of the heavenly host," which proclaims:

"Glory to God in the highest,
And on earth peace, good will toward men"

—or as the *New English Bible*, less poetically but perhaps more accurately, puts it:

"Glory to God in highest heaven,
And on earth his peace for men on whom
his favour rests."

If the military choirs of heaven sang the first
Christmas greeting, earthly men have ever since
been busy celebrating the event of Christmas in
endlessly varied poetry. The human chorus of cele-
bration has not been limited to professed Christians.
To the Christian the lowly manger may be, most of
all, the spot where God's reality is focused and
revealed in the face of a tiny baby, but to all men,
Christian or not, there is something about the
familiar tale that will not let go of them.

Certainly the poets in this little book are an ecu-
menical council in the broadest sense. Many shades
of Christians are here, but the Jewish voice is also
heard, and that of free-wheeling mystics and out-
right agnostics. No attempt has been made to select
only those poems composed by the orthodox and
the traditionally devout. The sole criterion is that
each poem say something about the birth of Christ
or Christmas, and say it well.

In time they range from about 1500 to the
present; one of the poems was written less than a
month before this manuscript was put in final form.
The temptation was great to include many of the
lovely medieval lyrics, but almost without excep-
tion these demand formidable scholarly apparatus
to make them accessible for the nonspecialist. About
half the space is given over to earlier centuries,

particularly the sixteenth and seventeenth, which are a golden age of Nativity poetry. The eighteenth and nineteenth centuries are more sparsely represented. For reasons that may best be left to the literary historians, the period is curiously barren of good Christmas poems, though abounding in bad ones.

Equal space is devoted to the twentieth century, which—it may come as a surprise to some—is comparable to the seventeenth century in the abundance and quality of Christmas poems. But our century has many moods, bitter as well as sweet. Arnold Kenseth can strike the note of adoration as singly and purely as any seventeenth-century poet, but many of his contemporaries write not so much Christmas poems as "anti-Christmas poems." Lawrence Ferlinghetti in "Christ Climbed Down" launches a savage assault on the commercialization of Christmas and sympathetically depicts Jesus as running away to where "there were no gilded Christmas trees." Bink Noll, in a gentler mood, spoofs the traditional Sunday School pageant. Thomas Hardy wistfully confesses that if someone told him the oxen were kneeling in their stall on Christmas Eve he would go there, "Hoping it might be so." To W. B. Yeats, Christmas suggests both the wonder that Mary experienced when she knew she had been set apart to bear Christ ("The Mother of God") and the thought that the Christian era may be drawing to an end and a new age of savage violence coming to birth ("The Second Coming").

The poems that at first glance seem the least devout often turn out to express—negatively, it may be—the most intense conviction of what Christmas ought to mean and be. At any rate, here is a garland of Christmas verse, nearly five hundred years of it, illustrating in many moods and poetic forms how deeply mankind is haunted by a single star in the sky, shepherds in the field, and most of all by one baby.

CHAD WALSH

Beloit College

GARLANDS FOR CHRISTMAS

FROM *Two Christmas-Cards*

For an hour on Christmas eve
And again on the holy day,
Seek the magic of past time,
From this present turn away.
Dark though our day,
Light lies the snow on the hawthorn hedges
And the ox knelt down at midnight.

Only an hour, only an hour
From wars and confusions turn away
To the islands of old time
When the world was simple and gay,
Or so we say,
And light lay the snow on the green holly,
The tall oxen knelt at midnight.

Caesar and Herod shared the world
Sorrow over Bethlehem lay,
Iron the empire, brutal the time
Dark was that first Christmas day,
Light lay the snow on the mistletoe berries
And the ox knelt down at midnight.

An Adoration

In this snowfall season the birth
Of God's furious and tender Son
Gives us our holy days by fire. Earth
Cradles once more the hope that Eve
And her winter children will receive
The sunlit garden; because fear
Has no room in our Saviour's castle.

All love shepherds us. The pageant kings
Weep for us. In argent rings
Heaven's wild gabriels wrestle
For our very souls. What stables here
Is time for us to give our sin
The shape of kneeling, to perch seven
Times seventy singing robins

Of forgiveness on our tongues,
Blessing our enemies, that the bones
Which we have broken may rejoice.
No one is lost, not one, who yields
Himself to Christmas. The red ribbons
Of his grief adorn us. The voice
Of his mercy is heard in our fields.

To His Saviour, a Child;
a Present, by a Child

Go prettie child, and beare this Flower
Unto thy little Saviour;
And tell Him, by that Bud now blown,
He is the *Rose of Sharon* known:
When thou hast said so, stick it there
Upon his Bibb, or Stomacher:
And tell Him (for good handsell too)
That thou hast brought a Whistle new,
Made of a clean strait oaten reed,
To charme his cries (at time of need):
Tell Him, for Corall, thou hast none;
But if thou hadst, He sho'd have one;
But poore thou art, and knowne to be
Even as monilesse, as He.
Lastly, if thou canst win a kisse
From those mellifluous lips of his;
Then never take a second on,
To spoile the first impression.

FROM *For the Time Being*

MARY

O shut your bright eyes that mine must endanger
With their watchfulness; protected by its shade
Escape from my care: what can you discover
From my tender look but how to be afraid?
Love can but confirm the more it would deny.
   Close your bright eye.

Sleep. What have you learned from the womb that
      bore you
But an anxiety your Father cannot feel?
Sleep. What will the flesh that I gave do for you,
Or my mother love, but tempt you from His will?
Why was I chosen to teach His Son to weep?
   Little One, sleep.

Dream. In human dreams earth ascends to Heaven
Where no one need pray nor ever feel alone.
In your first few hours of life here, O have you
Chosen already what death must be your own?
How soon will you start on the Sorrowful Way?
   Dream while you may.

A Christmas Carol

Welcome, sweet Christmas, blest be the morn
That Christ our Saviour was born!
Earth's Redeemer, to save us from all danger,
And, as the Holy Record tells, born in a manger.

Chorus: Then ring, ring, Christmas bells,
Till your sweet music o'er the kingdom swells,
To warn the people to respect the morn
That Christ their Saviour was born.

The snow was on the ground when Christ was born,
And the Virgin Mary His mother felt very forlorn
As she lay in a horse's stall at a roadside inn,
Till Christ our Saviour was born to free us from sin.

Oh! think of the Virgin Mary as she lay
In a lowly stable on a bed of hay,
And angels watching o'er her till Christ was born,
Therefore all the people should respect Christmas
morn.

The way to respect Christmas time
Is not by drinking whisky or wine,
But to sing praises to God on Christmas morn
The time that Jesus Christ His Son was born;

Whom He sent into the world to save sinners from
    hell,
And by believing in Him in heaven we'll dwell;
Then blest be the morn that Christ was born,
Who can save us from hell, death, and scorn.

Then be warned, and respect the Saviour dear,
And treat with less respect the New Year,
And respect always the blessed morn
That Christ our Saviour was born.

For each new morn to the Christian is dear,
As well as the morn of the New Year,
And he thanks God for the light of each new morn,
Especially the morn that Christ was born.

Therefore, good people, be warned in time,
And on Christmas morn don't get drunk with wine,
But praise God above on Christmas morn,
Who sent His Son to save us from hell and scorn.

There the heavenly babe He lay
In a stall among a lot of hay,
While the Angel Host by Bethlehem
Sang a beautiful and heavenly anthem.

Christmas time ought to be held most dear,
Much more so than the New Year,
Because that's the time that Christ was born,
Therefore respect Christmas morn.

And let the rich be kind to the poor,
And think of the hardships they do endure,
Who are neither clothed nor fed,
And many without a blanket to their bed.

New Heaven, New Warre

Come to your heaven you heavenly quires,
Earth hath the heaven of your desires;
Remove your dwelling to your God,
A stall is now his best abode;
Sith men their homage doe denie,
Come Angels all their fault supplie.

His chilling cold doth heate require,
Come Seraphins in liew of fire;
This little Arke no cover hath,
Let Cherubs wings his body swath:
Come Raphaell, this Babe must eate,
Provide our little Tobie meate.

Let Gabriell be now his groome,
That first took up his earthly roome;
Let Michaell stand in his defence,
Whom love hath linck'd to feeble sence,
Let Graces rock when he doth crie,
And Angels sing his lullabie.

The same you saw in heavenly seate,
Is he that now sucks Maries teate;
Agnize your King a mortall wight,
His borrowed weede lets not your sight:
Come kisse the maunger where he lies,
That is your blisse above the skies.

This little Babe so few dayes olde,
Is come to ryfle sathans folde;
All hell doth at his presence quake,
Though he himselfe for cold doe shake:
For in this weake unarmed wise,
The gates of hell he will suprise.

With teares he fights and winnes the field,
His naked breast stands for a shield;
His battering shot are babish cryes,
His Arrowes lookes of weeping eyes,
His Martiall ensignes cold and neede,
And feeble flesh his warriers steede.

His Campe is pitched in a stall,
His bulwarke but a broken wall:
The Crib his trench, hay stalks his stakes,
Of Sheepheards he his Muster makes;
And thus as sure his foe to wound,
The Angells trumps alarum sound.

My soule with Christ joyne thou in fight,
Sticke to the tents that he hath pight;
Within his Crib is surest ward,
This little Babe will be thy guard:
If thou wilt foyle thy foes with joy,
Then flit not from this heavenly boy.

Christmas

The bells of waiting Advent ring,
  The Tortoise stove is lit again
And lamp-oil light across the night
  Has caught the streaks of winter rain
In many a stained-glass window sheen
From Crimson Lake to Hooker's Green.

The holly in the windy hedge
  And round the Manor House the yew
Will soon be stripped to deck the ledge,
  The altar, font and arch and pew,
So that the villagers can say
"The church looks nice" on Christmas Day.

Provincial public houses blaze
  And Corporation tramcars clang,
On lighted tenements I gaze
  Where paper decorations hang,
And bunting in the red Town Hall
Says "Merry Christmas to you all."

And London shops on Christmas Eve
  Are strung with silver bells and flowers
As hurrying clerks the City leave
  To pigeon-haunted classic towers,
And marbled clouds go scudding by
The many-steepled London sky.

And girls in slacks remember Dad,
  And oafish louts remember Mum,
And sleepless children's hearts are glad,
  And Christmas-morning bells say "Come!"
Even to shining ones who dwell
Safe in the Dorchester Hotel.

And is it true? And is it true,
  This most tremendous tale of all,
Seen in a stained-glass window's hue,
  A Baby in an ox's stall?
The Maker of the stars and sea
Become a Child on earth for me?

And is it true? For if it is,
  No loving fingers tying strings
Around those tissued fripperies,
  The sweet and silly Christmas things,
Bath salts and inexpensive scent
And hideous tie so kindly meant,

No love that in a family dwells,
  No carolling in frosty air,
Nor all the steeple-shaking bells
  Can with this single Truth compare—
That God was Man in Palestine
And lives to-day in Bread and Wine.

FROM *Hamlet*

Some say that ever 'gainst that season comes
Wherein our Saviour's birth is celebrated,
This bird of dawning singeth all night long;
And then, they say, no spirit dare stir abroad,
The nights are wholesome, then no planets strike,
No fairy takes, nor witch hath power to charm,
So hallow'd and so gracious is the time.

The Oxen

Christmas Eve, and twelve of the clock.
  "Now they are all on their knees,"
An elder said as we sat in a flock
  By the embers in hearthside ease.

We pictured the meek mild creatures where
  They dwelt in their strawy pen,
Nor did it occur to one of us there
  To doubt they were kneeling then.

So fair a fancy few would weave
  In these years! Yet, I feel,
If someone said on Christmas Eve,
  "Come; see the oxen kneel

"In the lonely barton by yonder coomb
  Our childhood used to know,"
I should go with him in the gloom,
  Hoping it might be so.

FROM *In the Clearing*

But God's own descent
Into flesh was meant
As a demonstration
That the supreme merit
Lay in risking spirit
In substantiation.
Spirit enters flesh
And for all it's worth
Charges into earth
In birth after birth
Ever fresh and fresh.
We may take the view
That its derring-do
Thought of in the large
Is one mighty charge
On our human part
Of the soul's ethereal
Into the material.

The Nativitie of Christ

Beholde the father, is his daughters sonne:
The bird that built the nest, is hatched therein:
The olde of yeares, an houre hath not out runne:
Eternall life, to live doth now beginne.
The word is dumme: the mirth of heaven doth
    weepe:
Might feeble is: and force doth faintly creepe.

O dying soules, beholde your living spring:
O dasled eyes, behold your sonne of grace:
Dull eares, attend what word this word doth bring:
Up heavie hartes: with joye your joye embrace.
From death, from darke, from deafenesse, from
    dispaires:
This life, this light, this word, this joy repaires.

Gift better then himselfe, God doth not know:
Gift better then his God, no man can see:
This gift doth here the gever geven bestow:
Gift to this gift let each receiver bee.
God is my gift, himselfe he freely gave me:
Gods gift am I, and none but God shall have me.

Man altered was by sinne from man to beast:
Beastes foode is haye, haye is all mortall flesh:
Now God is flesh, and lies in Manger prest:
As haye, the brutest sinner to refresh.
O happie fielde wherein this fodder grew,
Whose tast, doth us from beasts to men renew.

Welcoming Poem for the Birth of My Son

Bubbling and bouncing, lumbering amid
The tickle of little fishes, whales
Jostle the sea; they are blubber balloons
Sailing their bodies' happiness, spouting
Hallelujah to the applause of seals,
The memoranda of walrusses, while
In the daft radiance of arctic noon,
Emperor penguins gather, for whom, as always,
It is opening night.

                Again, this blazing noon,
The play begins: reindeer gazing eastward
Raise their dazed eyes, jaws in their poised heads
Still sluicing lichen juices, they gaze beyond hunger
In first wonder of wet light, dreaming
What is there, while whales are blooming,
While walrusses are making lists for Christmas,
And emperor penguins parade their new clothes
Through the white meadow, the sun-struck king-
dom.

Up from the horizon, in purple depth,
Humped with porpoises; over the frozen sea
Where whales' bodies are blossoming games;
Past walrusses puckered to blow kisses,
Whiskered like Santa Claus; to the applause
Of seals fanning with their flippers the hot glaciers
In the zeal of their unbounded, bounding hearts—
He comes, all spirit, dressed in flesh and blood;
He comes, crowned in his cheeks and fuzz,
In a dazzle of fingers and toes, making miracles
With his glad eyes; he walks in a garden of penguins
Enraptured on their eggs, crying GOOD WILL
To that far city where my fears hide.

Nativitie

Immensity cloystered in thy deare wombe,
Now leaves his welbelov'd imprisonment,
There he hath made himselfe to his intent
Weake enough, now into our world to come;
But Oh, for thee, for him, hath th' Inne no roome?
Yet lay him in this stall, and from the Orient,
Starres, and wisemen will travell to prevent
Th' effect of *Herods* jealous generall doome.
Seest thou, my Soule, with thy faiths eyes, how he
Which fils all place, yet none holds him, doth lye?
Was not his pity towards thee wondrous high,
That would have need to be pittied by thee?
Kisse him, and with him into Egypt goe,
With his kinde mother, who partakes thy woe.

The Three Kings

Three Kings came riding from far away,
  Melchior and Gaspar and Baltasar;
Three Wise Men out of the East were they,
And they travelled by night and they slept by day,
  For their guide was a beautiful, wonderful star.

The star was so beautiful, large, and clear,
  That all the other stars of the sky
Became a white mist in the atmosphere,
And by this they knew that the coming was near
  Of the Prince foretold in the prophecy.

Three caskets they bore on their saddlebows,
  Three caskets of gold with golden keys;
Their robes were of crimson silk with rows
Of bells and pomegranates and furbelows,
  Their turbans like blossoming almond-trees.

And so the Three Kings rode into the West,
  Through the dusk of night, over hill and dell,
And sometimes they nodded with beard on breast,
And sometimes talked, as they paused to rest,
  With the people they met at some wayside well.

"Of the child that is born," said Baltasar,
  "Good people, I pray you, tell us the news;
For we in the East have seen his star,
And have ridden fast, and have ridden far,
  To find and worship the King of the Jews."

And the people answered, "You ask in vain;
  We know of no king but Herod the Great!"
They thought the Wise Men were men insane,
As they spurred their horses across the plain,
  Like riders in haste, and who cannot wait.

And when they came to Jerusalem,
  Herod the Great, who had heard this thing,
Sent for the Wise Men and questioned them;
And said, "Go down unto Bethlehem,
  And bring me tidings of this new king."

So they rode away; and the star stood still,
  The only one in the gray of morn;
Yes, it stopped, it stood still of its own free will,
Right over Bethlehem on the hill,
  The city of David where Christ was born.

And the Three Kings rode through the gate and
        the guard,
  Through the silent street, till their horses turned
And neighed as they entered the great inn-yard;
But the windows were closed, and the doors were
        barred,
  And only a light in the stable burned.

And cradled there in the scented hay,
  In the air made sweet by the breath of kine,
The little child in the manger lay,
The child, that would be king one day
  Of a kingdom not human but divine.

His mother Mary of Nazareth
  Sat watching beside his place of rest,
Watching the even flow of his breath,
For the joy of life and the terror of death
  Were mingled together in her breast.

They laid their offerings at his feet:
  The gold was their tribute to a King,
The frankincense, with its odor sweet,
Was for the Priest, the Paraclete,
  The myrrh for the body's burying.

And the mother wondered and bowed her head,
  And sat as still as a statue of stone;
Her heart was troubled yet comforted,
Remembering what the Angel had said
  Of an endless reign and of David's throne.

Then the Kings rode out of the city gate,
  With a clatter of hoofs in proud array;
But they went not back to Herod the Great,
For they knew his malice and feared his hate,
  And returned to their homes by another way.

Magi

They set out in bright approving summer:
flags, gold, imagination attending
down charted roads, the star like a sun of night,
and at earth's end, the unique King awaiting.

Autumn too was lovely and novel: weather tem-
    perate
and the star mellowing slowly as a moon.
Then winter on them: the light snuffed out:
hearsay, frontiers, men inimical to dreamers—
and what direction in iron snow?—a hind's track
diminished in ivory, a white birch stricken to
    ground
and the sky tolling its grey dispassionate bell
upon age, upon infinite heart's weariness.

So the great came, great only in need,
to the roof of thatch, the child at knee awaiting.

The Ballad of Befana

AN EPIPHANY LEGEND

Befana the Housewife, scrubbing her pane,
Saw three old sages ride down the lane,
Saw three gray travelers pass her door—
Gaspar, Balthazar, Melchior.

"Where journey you, sirs?" she asked of them.
Balthazar answered, "To Bethlehem,

For we have news of a marvelous thing.
Born in a stable is Christ the King."

"Give Him my welcome!"
Then Gaspar smiled,
"Come with us, mistress, to greet the Child."

"Oh, happily, happily would I fare,
Were my dusting through and I'd polished the
      stair."

Old Melchior leaned on his saddle horn.
"Then send but a gift to the small Newborn."

"Oh, gladly, gladly I'd send Him one,
Were the hearthstone swept and my weaving done.

"As soon as ever I've baked my bread,
I'll fetch Him a pillow for His head,
And a coverlet too," Befana said.

"When the rooms are aired and the linen dry,
I'll look at the Babe."
But the Three rode by.

She worked for a day and a night and a day,
Then, gifts in her hands, took up her way.
But she never could find where the Christ Child lay.

And still she wanders at Christmastide,
Houseless, whose house was all her pride,

Whose heart was tardy, whose gifts were late;
Wanders, and knocks at every gate,
Crying, "Good people, the bells begin!
Put off your toiling and let love in."

The Mother of God

The threefold terror of love; a fallen flare
Through the hollow of an ear;
Wings beating about the room;
The terror of all terrors that I bore
The Heavens in my womb.

Have I not found content among the shows
Every common woman knows,
Chimney corner, garden walk,
Or rocky cistern where we tread the clothes
And gather all the talk?

What is this flesh I purchased with my pains,
This fallen star my milk sustains,
This love that makes my heart's blood stop
Or strikes a sudden chill into my bones
And bids my hair stand up?

Letter to Santa Claus

Leap, Santa, down our chimney
With all-embracing fervour
In boots and beard so comely
Be now the red-checked saviour,
Volcano out your lava,

Where mixed with father's braces
And box of chocs for mother
Meccano sets build kisses
Where gliders lover each other
And sister flatters brother.

Dish out a world where tinsel
Spells laughter out in streamers
And gift propelling-pencil
Makes poems up for dreamers
And writes all wrong for schemers.

The chance we had the feeling
Was ours just for the knocking
Before we started quailing
At warnings old but shocking:
Just drop it in the stocking.

Give, Santa, give! Our needs
Have grown too great to measure;
Give cufflinks, lovers, beads,
Give tricycles, give pleasure,
Give Mother, God, and leisure.

We promise in return
To bless your boots and whiskers
And always to confirm
Reports of your existence
And be your careless friskers:
Heed, Santa, our insistence,
No longer keep your distance!

Dürer's Nativity

Dürer in woodcuts blacked-lined in
Two worlds and almost made them one:
Blazed heaven down on Bethlehem,
Turreted mad Jerusalem
Up into clouds, and hung God's graces
In doves above his peasants' faces.
He read the pouted lips of sin
Even in those who praised the Son.

So he drew Mary plain and round
As any mother-Mary found;
Cut barn beams, straw, in blocks of wood,
Doffed Dick the shepherd's steepled hat
In foolish love. The horned ox stood
Watching God's poverty asleep.
God's wisdom, then, is simply that
The lowly may accept the deep.

Albrecht, this meek festivity
Under the stable's broken roof,
Where tiered-winged angels kneel in love
And dimpled cherubs choir in rings,
Claims us. We cannot stand aloof.
We pray for the descending dove,
The grace of the enfolding wings
On this and all nativity.

Nativity

PIERO DELLA FRANCESCA

O cruel cloudless space,
And pale bare ground where the poor infant lies!
Why do we feel restored
As in a sacramental place?
Here Mystery is taking place
And here a vision of such peace is stored
Healing flows from it through our eyes.

Comfort and joy are near,
Not as we know them in the usual ways,
Personal and expected,
But utterly distilled and spare
Like a cool breath upon the air.
Emotion, it would seem, has been rejected
For a clear geometric praise.

Even the angels' stance
Is architectural in form,
And they tell no story.
We see on each grave countenance,
Withheld as in a formal dance,
The awful joy, the serene glory:
It is the inscape keeps us warm.

Poised as a monument,
Thought rests, and in these balanced spaces
Images meditate;
Whatever Piero meant,
The strange impersonal does not relent:
Here is love, naked, lying in great state
On the bare ground, as in all human faces.

A Christmas Carol

The shepherds went their hasty way,
   And found the lowly stable-shed
Where the Virgin-Mother lay:
   And now they checked their eager tread,
For to the Babe, that at her bosom clung,
A Mother's song the Virgin-Mother sung.

They told her how a glorious light,
   Streaming from a heavenly throng,
Around them shone, suspending night!
   While sweeter than a mother's song,
Blest Angels heralded the Saviour's birth,
Glory to God on high! and Peace on Earth.

She listened to the tale divine,
   And closer still the Babe she pressed;
And while she cried, the Babe is mine!
   The milk rushed faster to her breast:
Joy rose within her, like a summer's morn;
Peace, Peace on Earth! the Prince of Peace is born.

Thou Mother of the Prince of Peace,
    Poor, simple, and of low estate!
That strife should vanish, battle cease,
    O why should this thy soul elate?
Sweet Music's loudest note, the Poet's story—
Didst thou ne'er love to hear of fame and glory?

And is not War a youthful king,
    A stately Hero clad in mail?
Beneath his footsteps laurels spring;
    Him Earth's majestic monarchs hail
Their friend, their playmate! and his bold bright eye
Compels the maiden's love-confessing sigh.

"Tell this in some more courtly scene,
    To maids and youths in robes of state!
I am a woman poor and mean,
    And therefore is my soul elate.
War is a ruffian, all with guilt defiled,
That from the aged father tears his child!

"A murderous fiend, by fiends adored,
    He kills the sire and starves the son;
The husband kills, and from her board
    Steals all his widow's toil had won;
Plunders God's world of beauty; rends away
All safety from the night, all comfort from the day.

"Then wisely is my soul elate,
    That strife should vanish, battle cease:
I'm poor and of a low estate,
    The Mother of the Prince of Peace.
Joy rises in me, like a summer's morn:
Peace, Peace on Earth! the Prince of Peace is born."

Swedish Angel

The Swedish angel is nine inches high and shaped
    all of blond straw.
All of blond straw is her little body and her great
    seven-inch wings.
Her small head is of painted wood and she stands in
    a slim wood base.
Shining and shining in the Christmas candles,
    shines her golden halo.

Even all round her is a kind of shining, circle on
    circle, because
She has—as if—lighted upon a round lake of clear
    glass
Surrounded by ground-pine and red berries which
    gleam also
In the candlelight that moves on her stilled blond
    wings.

In this immaculate doll of heaven has been con-
    ceived, as though
No hands had shaped her, an uninvented innocence
    bequeathing grace
Ring upon ring in halos all around her, and not
    remote nor kind
But only there, dispensing of all the brought light a
    total larger light.

Even now her wings have assumed such shields of
    glory and the pool beneath
Wheels with such wreaths of shining, the room is
    gathered and filled
By her tall and burning stillness and, an actual
    angel, her suspension wars
For a whole minute against all the dark, as if I
    were a child.

Christ Climbed Down

Christ climbed down
from His bare Tree
this year
and ran away to where
there were no rootless Christmas trees
hung with candycanes and breakable stars

Christ climbed down
from His bare Tree
this year
and ran away to where
there were no gilded Christmas trees
and no tinsel Christmas trees
and no tinfoil Christmas trees
and no pink plastic Christmas trees
and no gold Christmas trees
and no black Christmas trees
and no powderblue Christmas trees
hung with electric candles
and encircled by tin electric trains
and clever cornball relatives

Christ climbed down
from His bare Tree
this year
and ran away to where
no intrepid Bible salesmen
covered the territory
in two-tone cadillacs
and where no Sears Roebuck creches
complete with plastic babe in manger
arrived by parcel post
the babe by special delivery
and where no televised Wise Men
praised the Lord Calvert Whiskey

Christ climbed down
from His bare Tree
this year
and ran away to where
no fat handshaking stranger
in a red flannel suit
and a fake white beard
went around passing himself off
as some sort of North Pole saint
crossing the desert to Bethlehem
Pennsylvania
in a Volkswagon sled
drawn by rollicking Adirondack reindeer
with German names

and bearing sacks of Humble Gifts
from Saks Fifth Avenue
for everybody's imagined Christ child

Christ climbed down
from His bare Tree
this year
and ran away to where
no Bing Crosby carollers
groaned of a tight Christmas
and where no Radio City angels
iceskated wingless
thru a winter wonderland
into a jinglebell heaven
daily at 8:30
with Midnight Mass matinees

Christ climbed down
from His bare Tree
this year
and softly stole away into
some anonymous Mary's womb again
where in the darkest night
of everybody's anonymous soul
He awaits again
an unimaginable
and impossibly
Immaculate Reconception
the very craziest
of Second Comings

In the Kindergarten

Miss Cadbury's epiphanies occur
yearly where newfledged cherubs flock
on platforms lugged here by the janitor

who also brings out the same box
full of carols, cheesecloth wings, cheap
velvet, sheets, Christ doll & other props.

Nostrils full of chalk—week after week,
she trains her pupils to show their parents
a miracle of shepherds without sheep.

Stiff-robed they stray into the sequence
strange as freaks, at last spy the god—
these three crowned dwarfs—and cap sublime events.

Each brings a vacant, castoff pot,
for what's frankincense now? or myrrh?
Today kings walk into the plot

from giggling in the corridor.

A Christmas Carroll

So, now is come our joyfulst *Feast*;
Let ever man be jolly.
Each Roome, with Ivie leaves is drest,
And every Post, with Holly.
    Though some Churles at our mirth repine,
    Round your foreheads Garlands twine,
    Drowne sorrow in a Cup of Wine.
And let us all be merry.

Now, all our Neighbours Chimneys smoke,
And *Christmas* blocks are burning;
Their Ovens, they with bakt-meats choke,
And all their Spits are turning.
    Without the doore, let sorrow lie:
    And, if for cold, it hap to die,
    We'll bury 't in a *Christmas* Pie.
And evermore be merry.

Now, every *Lad* is wondrous trim,
And no man minds his Labour.
Our Lasses have provided them,

A Bag-pipe, and a Tabor.
 Young men, and Mayds, and Girles & Boyes,
 Give life, to one anothers Joyes:
 And, you anon shall by their noyse,
Perceive that they are merry.

Ranke Misers now, doe sparing shun:
Their Hall of Musicke soundeth:
And, Dogs, thence with whole shoulders run,
So, all things there aboundeth.
 The Countrey-folke, themselves advance;
 For *Crowdy-Mutton's* come out of *France*:
 And *Jack* shall pipe, and *Jill* shall dance,
And all the Towne be merry.

Ned Swash hath fetcht his Bands from pawne,
And all his best Apparell.
Brisk *Nell* hath brought a Ruffe of Lawne,
With droppings of the Barrell.
 And those that hardly all the yeare
 Had Bread to eat, or Raggs to weare,
 Will have both Clothes, and daintie fare:
And all the day be merry.

Now poore men to the *Justices*,
With Capons make their arrants,
And if they hap to faile of these,
They plague them with their Warrants.
 But now they feed them with good cheere,
 And what they want, they take in Beere:

For, Christmas *comes but once a yeare*:
And then they shall be merry.

Good *Farmers*, in the Country, nurse
The poore, that else were undone.
Some *Land*-lords, spend their money worse
On Lust, and Pride at *London*.
   There, the Roysters they doe play;
   Drabb and Dice their Lands away,
   Which may be ours, another day:
And therefore let's be merry.

The Client now his suit forbeares,
The Prisoners heart is eased,
The Debtor drinks away his cares,
And, for the time is pleased.
   Though others purses be more fat,
   Why should we pine or grieve at that?
   Hang sorrow, care will kill a Cat.
And therefore let's be merry.

Harke, how the *Wagges*, abroad doe call
Each other foorth to rambling.
Anon, you'll see them in the Hall,
For Nuts, and Apples scambling.
   Harke, how the Roofes with laughters sound
   Anon they'll thinke the house goes round:
   For, they the Cellars depth have found.
And there they will be merry.

The *Wenches* with their *Wassell-Bowles*,
About the Streets are singing:
The *Boyes* are come to catch the *Owles*,
The *Wild-mare*, in is bringing.
    Our *Kitchin-Boy* hath broke his Boxe,
    And, to the dealing of the Oxe,
    Our honest neighbours come by flocks,
And here they will be merry.

Now *Kings* and *Queenes*, poore Sheep-cotes have,
And mate with every body:
The honest, now, may play the *knave*,
And wise men play at *Noddy*.
    Some Youths will now a *Mumming* goe;
    Some others play at *Rowland-hoe*,
    And, twenty other Gameboyes moe:
Because they will be merry.

Then wherefore in these merry daies,
Should we I pray, be duller?
No; let us sing some *Roundelayes*,
To make our mirth the fuller.
    And, whilest thus inspir'd we sing,
    Let all the Streets with ecchoes ring:
    Woods, and Hills, and every thing,
Beare witnesse we are merry.

Posada

(For reading by groups, during the ten days before Christmas)

MARY:

Go, Joseph, knock! O knock again!
  Again knock on the Door!

SATAN:

That this all-labouring world of pain
  Need travel on no more.

GABRIEL:

That what will be may be
And what must be can be
That what could be should be.

MARY:

Yet, yet, again! Knock on again!
  Again knock on the Door!

SATAN:

That this nigh-foundering race of men
  Learn what the sword is for.

JOSEPH:

So I, despairing, hammer on my heart.
　O open, open wide and let blow in
The unsparing Word that chose me for this part,
　Filling this void that's hunger and that's sin.

PORTER:

Knock at this hour! Be off, you there!
　Why should we find you room!
No opening now, for pay nor prayer.
　Think you're the crack of doom!

They come by day the folk that we let in
　To take their ease, for light and food and sleep.
This Door won't open now for all your din.
　An Inn's an Inn and not a fortress keep.

INNKEEPER:

This night's not like another night.
　Some THING's abroad I doubt.
My porter there is in the right
　To keep these vagrants out.

GUEST IN THE INN:

Slow and cold, dust blowing all the way:
　Wind-burn parched and foot and saddle sore.
A ruinous place but still a place to stay.
　What's all that argie-bargie at the Door?

ANOTHER GUEST:

Snug here! Let's hope those batterings at the Door
  Don't mean the You Know Who have caught us
      up!
I had as lief not fight it out once more.
  Meanwhile we may as well fill up the cup.

SERVING WENCH:

A pinchy lot to serve their meat and drink,
  Smile at, be saucy with—and sometimes more:
At beck and call to any nod or wink.
  Ah, that young lad so haggard at the Door.

ANOTHER GUEST:

Good pickings maybe. No pig in a poke.
  Some chance at least to see which of them's which.
Who wants to waste his talents on the broke?
  So here's our bumper toast: "God Save the Rich!"

ANOTHER GUEST:

It's just as well we left the pearls behind.
  Don't too much like the looks of some of these.
Better not seem to have it on your mind.
  These gentry's style in arguing isn't "Please!"

ANOTHER GUEST:

Stony the waste and blinding chill the wind,
  Secretive and hid the passers-by.
Men get more talkative when they have dined,
  Grow less inclined to take you for a spy.

JOSEPH:

What Inn is this? So pitiless its Door,
   It will not hark or heed;
It will not hear however I implore;
   It will not even let me show the Need.

O more than life to me, so not my life;
   Why on you, why should this on you be laid,
O my betrothed, my partner not my wife?
   What doom is this set on an honest maid?

FIRST NEIGHBOUR:

She looks too good to be in such a plight.
   Demure yet proud. Uppish, no doubt.
But now she comes to learn what serves her right:
   In such a night as this to be shut out!

SECOND NEIGHBOUR:

Nothing but riff-raff, flotsam of the Ways,
   Improvident and feckless are the poor!
Without the wit even to count the days.
   Then go and knock on any decent door!

DONKEY:

Hee-haw! See-saw! She's had her fun and fling!
   And now it's all caught up with her at last.
She must have been the doxy of a King;
   Not that poor chap so helpless and aghast.

SATAN:

Here is my cue to play the Morning Star!
   Too big she is to weather out the night.
I'll show them where the hay and manger are.
   Follow me now, all Power and all Might.

GABRIEL:

Helpful as ever the Adversary is,
   Alert to forward what he calls his plan.
The very first to think he knows what's his,
   Acting his part out between God and man.

      That what will be may be
      And what must be can be
      That what could be should be.

For Daphne at Christmas

Christmas again. And the kings. And the camels that
    Travel like shanties collapsing. We hurl
      Fistfuls of shivery bliss in the night on a
        Tree that runs fall-color, breathes of a girl.

Men had a myth: how Apollo (no kin of mine)
    Flushing in shrubs a bent shoulder and head,
      Snorted and plunged for her, lofty blood thun-
          dering—
        "Oh," she said. *"Oh!"* she said. There's a
          girl sped.

Hovered high hurdles; flashed a fine knee or so,
    Flashed a fine—Ovid says, how her flounce flew.
      Cornered, she crinkled to armfuls of laurel, her
        Heartbeat in bark ebbing. Likely: I knew

Much the same story: once scuffled fall foliage;
    Caught the soft runaway, crushed to my brow
      Curls that turned holly-leaves, pin-pointy, hiss-
          ing things;
        Felt the warm bark alive. Heaven knows how

These had gone walking all the broad autumn,
  Poked in gold cubby-holes down the dark run;
    Fumbled in foliage crisp as old tinsel, and
      Tussled and scuffed too much. Blurting:
        "Been fun."

Fun!—but it wasn't fun. Blundered half purposely
  Into each other—through wool such delight?
    "I want you all," he choked, "cornflower, corn-
        tassel!"
      "Oh," she laughed, redder then. "*Oh!*" she
        wept, white.

"Snug rough and tumble here? Fun in a furrow
        bunk?
  What would you do, gamin? Turn to a tree?"
    "I don't know." Tears flickered. "I don't
        know." Hems flinging.
      Whitely defiant though: "Try. And you'll
        see."

Down the dense calendar's black and red stubble
        field
  Gone, the October girl. Plunging, he kept
    Eyes on a—cypress? Dead mistletoe? Myrtle-
        bush?
      Oak that had crashed on him? Willow that
        wept?

Ashen as sassifras? Judas-tree? Juniper?
　Trekking November, he scuffed the dull days.
　　Pinned her at Christmas, in cedar gloom
　　　wassailing.
　　　Sombre, and swirling dark rum as she sways:

"What's a gone girl to you? Better: forever-things.
　All the fall-forest bit; all the dense kiss.
　　Look, I'm a tree." She spun tasselled with tinsel,
　　　and
　　　Pinned, in her pony-tail, tree-glitter: "This

Crimson for lips, the fall foliage ranting;
　Gold for that foliage blurred the wind's bliss.
　　Blue, for dense gloom in the cornstubble star-
　　　light;
　　　Silver—for lashes lay salt to the kiss.

Better a tree. So embrace me, I'll do for you."
　Arms like boughs bending, she downed the dark
　　　rum.
　　"Better a year-spirit. Others have summer.
　　　But
　　　Mine, when the kings and the camel-train
　　　come."

The Lamb

Little Lamb, who made thee,
Dost thou know who made thee,
Gave thee life, and bade thee feed
By the stream and o'er the mead;
Gave thee clothing of delight,
Softest clothing, woolly, bright;
Gave thee such a tender voice,
Making all the vales rejoice?
  Little Lamb, who made thee?
  Dost thou know who made thee?

Little Lamb, I'll tell thee;
Little Lamb, I'll tell thee:
He is callèd by thy name,
For He calls himself a Lamb.
He is meek, and He is mild,
He became a little child.
I a child, and thou a lamb,
We are callèd by His name.
  Little Lamb, God bless thee!
  Little Lamb, God bless thee!

A Christmas Carol

(The chief constable has issued a statement declaring that carol singing in the streets by children is illegal, and morally and physically injurious. He appeals to the public to discourage the practice.—
DAILY PAPER*)*

> God rest you merry gentlemen,
> Let nothing you dismay;
> The Herald Angels cannot sing,
> The cops arrest them on the wing,
> And warn them of the docketing
> Of anything they say.
>
> God rest you merry gentlemen,
> May nothing you dismay:
> On your reposeful cities lie
> Deep silence, broken only by
> The motor horn's melodious cry,
> The hooter's happy bray.

So, when the song of children ceased
And Herod was obeyed,
In his high hall Corinthian
With purple and with peacock fan,
Rested that merry gentleman;
And nothing him dismayed.

The Mystic's Christmas

"All hail!" the bells of Christmas rang,
"All hail!" the monks at Christmas sang,
The merry monks who kept with cheer
The gladdest day of all their year.

But still apart, unmoved thereat,
A pious elder brother sat
Silent, in his accustomed place,
With God's sweet peace upon his face.

"Why sitt'st thou thus?" his brethren cried.
"It is the blessed Christmas-tide;
The Christmas lights are all aglow,
The sacred lilies bud and blow.

"Above our heads the joy-bells ring,
Without the happy children sing,
And all God's creatures hail the morn
On which the holy Christ was born!

"Rejoice with us; no more rebuke
Our gladness with thy quiet look."
The gray monk answered: "Keep, I pray,
Even as ye list, the Lord's birthday.

"Let heathen Yule fires flicker red
Where thronged refectory feasts are spread;
With mystery-play and masque and mime
And wait-songs speed the holy time!

"The blindest faith may haply save;
The Lord accepts the things we have;
And reverence, howsoe'er it strays,
May find at last the shining ways.

"They needs must grope who cannot see,
The blade before the ear must be;
As ye are feeling I have felt,
And where ye dwell I too have dwelt.

"But now, beyond the things of sense,
Beyond occasions and events,
I know, through God's exceeding grace,
Release from form and time and place.

"I listen, from no mortal tongue,
To hear the song the angels sung;
And wait within myself to know
The Christmas lilies bud and blow.

"The outward symbols disappear
From him whose inward sight is clear;
And small must be the choice of days
To him who fills them all with praise!

"Keep while you need it, brothers mine,
With honest zeal your Christmas sign,
But judge not him who every morn
Feels in his heart the Lord Christ born!"

Annunciation

A women knows when the seed
Is sown. As the furled earth
Curves in a wave, and the treed
Bird sings the spring to birth,
The amazed seed explores the dark.
Mary hailed the seed and the lark.

The savage swan took Leda in flight,
Semele bore the scars of Zeus;
Mary conceived a beam of light,
And later, with robes flowing loose,
The gravid woman in star-riveted night
Felt the growth of the Son of Light.

"Hail to Thee, my God-given Son,
Hail to Thee and to Thy fate.
You shape the shape of the world to come;
I hear you knocking at my soft gate."

A woman knows when her time is near.
When the ebb flows, the waters rush out,
Away from the caverns, away from the sheer
Cliffs. The sea-birds cry and flout
The wind. The stranded starfish is amazed.
Mary hailed the child and gazed.

The women of Greece bore the children of gods.
The woman of grace bore the Child of God.
The children of Greece were killed when trod
Under Troy's heavy foot, but Christ was crossed
Upon the tree. They stretched his bones,
But they set him free.

Hail to Thee, God-shaped Son,
Hail to Mary and to Thy fate.
Hail to death and nativity;
I hear soft knocking at our hard gate.

Christmas

dirty Christmas
which Origen
and Clement
both showed up

for the junk it
is—as though,
sd O, he was a
mere Pharaoh. Or,

says Clement, do
we have here some
child baptism to
go gew-gaw over?

in long favorably
embroidered gown,
a boy? instead of
a man standing

in desire in the
Jordan, with green
banks on either
side, a naked man

treated by another
adult man who also
has found out that
to be as harmless

as a dove is what
a man gets as wise
as a serpent for,
the river,

of life?

Christmas

Christmas has come, let's eat and drink—
This is no time to sit and think;
Farewell to study, books and pen,
And welcome to all kinds of men.
Let all men now get rid of care,
And what one has let others share;
Then 'tis the same, no matter which
Of us is poor, or which is rich.
Let each man have enough this day,
Since those that can are glad to pay;
There's nothing now too rich or good
For poor men, not the King's own food.
Now like a singing bird my feet
Touch earth, and I must drink and eat.
Welcome to all men: I'll not care
What any of my fellows wear;
We'll not let cloth divide our souls,
They'll swim stark naked in the bowls.
Welcome, poor beggar: I'll not see
That hand of yours dislodge a flea—
While you sit at my side and beg,

Or right foot scratching your left leg.
Farewell restraint: we will not now
Measure the ale our brains allow,
But drink as much as we can hold.
We'll count no change when we spend gold;
This is no time to save, but spend,
To give for nothing, not to lend.
Let foes make friends: let them forget
The mischief-making dead that fret
The living with complaint like this—
"He wronged us once, hate him and his."
Christmas has come; let every man
Eat, drink, be merry all he can.
Ale's my best mark, but if port wine
Or whisky's yours—let it be mine;
No matter what lies in the bowls,
We'll make it rich with our own souls.
Farewell to study, books and pen,
And welcome to all kinds of men.

Christmas

All after pleasures as I rid one day,
  My horse and I, both tir'd, bodie and minde,
  With full crie of affections, quite astray,
I took up in the next inne I could finde.
There when I came, whom found I but my deare,
  My dearest Lord, expecting till the grief
  Of pleasures brought me to him, readie there
To be all passengers most sweet relief?
O Thou, whose glorious, yet contracted light,
  Wrapt in nights mantle, stole into a manger;
  Since my dark soul and brutish is thy right,
To Man of all beasts be thou not a stranger:
  Furnish & deck my soul, that thou mayst have
  A better lodging then a rack or grave.

The shepherds sing; and shall I silent be?
       My God, no hymne for thee?
My soul's a shepherd too; a flock it feeds
       Of thoughts, and words, and deeds.
The pasture is thy word: the streams, thy grace
       Enriching all the place.

Shepherd and flock shall sing, and all my powers
  Out-sing the day-light houres.
Then we will chide the sunne for letting night
  Take up his place and right:
We sing one common Lord; wherefore he should
  Himself the candle hold.
I will go searching, till I finde a sunne
  Shall stay, till we have done;
A willing shiner, that shall shine as gladly,
  As frost-nipt sunnes look sadly.
Then we will sing, and shine all our own day,
  And one another pay:
His beams shall cheer my breast, and both so twine,
Till ev'n his beams sing, and my musick shine.

The Second Coming

Turning and turning in the widening gyre
The falcon cannot hear the falconer;
Things fall apart; the centre cannot hold;
Mere anarchy is loosed upon the world,
The blood-dimmed tide is loosed, and everywhere
The ceremony of innocence is drowned;
The best lack all conviction, while the worst
Are full of passionate intensity.

Surely some revelation is at hand;
Surely the Second Coming is at hand.
The Second Coming! Hardly are those words out
When a vast image out of *Spiritus Mundi*
Troubles my sight: somewhere in sands of the desert
A shape with lion body and the head of a man,
A gaze blank and pitiless as the sun,
Is moving its slow thighs, while all about it
Reel shadows of the indignant desert birds.
The darkness drops again; but now I know

That twenty centuries of stony sleep
Were vexed to nightmare by a rocking cradle,
And what rough beast, its hour come round at last,
Slouches towards Bethlehem to be born?

Hymn XXXII: *The Nativity of Our Lord and Saviour Jesus Christ*

Where is this stupendous stranger,
    Swains of Solyma, advise,
Lead me to my Master's manger,
    Shew me where my Saviour lies?

O Most Mighty! O Most Holy!
    Far beyond the seraph's thought,
Art thou then so mean and lowly
    As unheeded prophets taught?

O the magnitude of meekness!
    Worth from worth immortal sprung;
O the strength of infant weakness,
    If eternal is so young!

If so young and thus eternal,
    Michael tune the shepherd's reed,
Where the scenes are ever vernal,
    And the loves be love indeed!

See the God blasphem'd and doubted
    In the schools of Greece and Rome;
See the pow'rs of darkness routed,
    Taken at their utmost gloom.

Nature's decorations glisten
    Far above their usual trim;
Birds on box and laurel listen,
    As so near the cherubs hymn.

Boreas now no longer winters
    On the desolated coast;
Oaks no more are riv'n in splinters
    By the whirlwind and his host.

Spinks and ouzels sing sublimely,
    "We too have a Saviour born";
Whiter blossoms burst untimely
    On the blest Mosaic thorn.

God all-bounteous, all-creative,
    Whom no ills from good dissuade,
Is incarnate, and a native
    Of the very world he made.

Ecce Puer

Of the dark past
A child is born
With joy and grief
My heart is torn

Calm in his cradle
The living lies.
May love and mercy
Unclose his eyes!

Young life is breathed
On the glass;
The world that was not
Comes to pass.

A child is sleeping:
An old man gone.
O father forsaken,
Forgive your son!

Santa Claus

Somewhere on his travels the strange Child
Picked up with this overstuffed confidence man,
Affection's inverted thief, who climbs at night
Down chimneys, into dreams, with this world's
    goods.
Bringing all the benevolence of money,
He teaches the innocent to want, thus keeps
Our fat world rolling. His prescribed costume,
White flannel beard, red belly of cotton waste,
Conceals the thinness of essential hunger,
An appetite that feeds on satisfaction;
Or, pregnant with possessions, he brings forth
Vanity and the void. His name itself
Is corrupted, and even Saint Nicholas, in his turn,
Gives off a faint and reminiscent stench,
The merest soupçon, of brimstone and the pit.

Now, at the season when the Child is born
To suffer for the world, suffer the world,
His bloated Other, jovial satellite
And sycophant, makes his appearance also

In a glitter of goodies, in a rock candy glare.
Played at the better stores by bums, for money,
This annual savior of the economy
Speaks in the parables of the dollar sign:
Suffer the little children to come to Him.

At Easter, he's anonymous again,
Just one of the crowd lunching on Calvary.

The Burning Babe

As I in hoarie Winters night
    Stoode shivering in the snow,
Surpris'd I was with sodaine heate,
    Which made my hart to glow;

And lifting up a fearefull eye,
    To view what fire was neare,
A pretty Babe all burning bright
    Did in the ayre appeare;

Who scorched with excessive heate,
    Such floods of teares did shed,
As though his floods should quench his flames,
    Which with his teares were fed:

Alas (quoth he) but newly borne,
    In fierie heates I frie,
Yet none approach to warme their harts
    Or feele my fire, but I;

My faultlesse breast the furnace is,
    The fuell wounding thornes:
Love is the fire, and sighs the smoake,
    The ashes, shame and scornes;

The fewell Justice layeth on,
    And Mercie blowes the coales,
The mettall in this furnace wrought,
    Are mens defiled soules:

For which, as now on fire I am
    To worke them to their good,
So will I melt into a bath,
    To wash them in my blood.

With this he vanisht out of sight,
    And swifty shrunk away,
And straight I called unto minde,
    That it was Christmasse day.

First Came Christmas

Christmas having been is Christmas come,
A sound too high to smother, light too firm
To crack for bev-count, coming as it came.

    Sprawled in vertigos of space
    Why should the space-drunk curse
    So mild an interference
    From a minor universe?

Gag the shepherds, skewer wise men, still
The infant comes, and someone sees and hears.
Bethlehem stands, needs neither star nor hill.
It houses Presence every Herod fears.

Eros and Dionysus span our days,
The plus and minus of time's tragedies;
But on this night the vast new murmurs rise.

Should scant accommodation
Within a drafty shed
Impel reverberation
Computers cannot read?

Neither bigots' lash nor suavest scorn
Deflects the rebel pulse no hate can tame.
Easter is Christmas first. And having come,
Forever now more valiant love is born.

The Invoice Clerk

The Invoice Clerk hasn't come today.
In the beginning was the Word
He gave no reason for being away.
And the Word was with God and the Word was God

He looked well enough. Was there fog on his line?
The same was in the beginning with God
It may be a question of discipline.
All that was made was made by him

Some think he is queer, the Invoice Clerk.
Without him was not anything made
He doesn't drink beer, the Invoice Clerk.
And his life was the light of men

Schofield and Roberts will move to Accounts.
And the light in the darkness shines
Block must authorise Debit Amounts.
And the darkness knows it not

Whether we take on another clerk
And the light in the darkness shines
Will depend on how these arrangements work.
And the darkness knows it not

Karma

Christmas was in the air and all was well
With him, but for a few confusing flaws
In divers of God's images. Because
A friend of his would neither buy nor sell,
Was he to answer for the axe that fell?
He pondered; and the reason for it was,
Partly, a slowly freezing Santa Claus
Upon the corner, with his beard and bell.

Acknowledging an improvident surprise,
He magnified a fancy that he wished
The friend whom he had wrecked were here again.
Not sure of that, he found a compromise;
And from the fulness of his heart he fished
A dime for Jesus who had died for men.

Christmas in Black Rock

Christ God's red shadow hangs upon the wall
The dead leaf's echo on these hours
Whose burden spindles to no breath at all;
Hard at our heels the huntress moonlight towers
And the green needles bristle at the glass
Tiers of defense-plants where the treadmill night
Churns up Long Island Sound with piston-fist.
Tonight, my child, the lifeless leaves will mass,
Heaving and heaping, as the swivelled light
Burns on the bell-spar in the fruitless mist.

Christ Child, your lips are lean and evergreen
Tonight in Black Rock, and the moon
Sidles outside into the needle-screen
And strikes the hand that feeds you with a spoon
Tonight, as drunken Polish night-shifts walk
Over the causeway and their juke-box booms
Hosannah in excelsis Domino.
Tonight, my child, the foot-loose hallows stalk
Us down in the blind alleys of our rooms;
By the mined root the leaves will overflow.

December, old leech, has leafed through Autumn's
    store
Where Poland has unleashed its dogs
To bay the moon upon the Black Rock shore:
Under our windows, on the rotten logs
The moonbeam, bobbing like an apple, snags
The undertow. O Christ, the spiralling years
Slither with child and manger to a ball
Of ice; and what is man? We tear our rags
To hang the Furies by their itching ears,
And the green needles nail us to the wall.

Christmas Mourning

On Christmas Day I weep
Good Friday to rejoice.
I watch the Child asleep.
Does He half dream the choice
The Man must make and keep?

At Christmastime I sigh
For my Good Friday hope.
Outflung the Child's arms lie
To span in their brief scope
The death the Man must die.

Come Christmastide I groan
To hear Good Friday's pealing.
The Man, racked to the bone,
Has made His hurt my healing,
Has made my ache His own.

Slay me, pierced to the core
With Christmas penitence
So I who, new-born, soar
To that Child's innocence,
May wound the Man no more.

Nativity

All creatures then rejoiced, save that the Seven
    Capital steers of whom I am a herder
      (My Cloven heart their hoofprint in the mire)
With bloodshot glare interrogated heaven,
    And, back, to back with lowered horns of murder
      From spiracles of fury spirted fire.

Never so joyfully the brave cocks crew—
    No more by turns, but all with one accord.
      Never so early woke the mule and ox
Since it was day before the east was blue:
    Mary was dawn, the Sunrise was our Lord,
      And Joseph was the watchtower on the rocks.

Never for such a golden quilt lay blooming,
    The fields, as for this richly laden hay,
      And though the frost was sharp before the day,
The mule and ox, whose respiration fuming
    Ignited in the lantern's dim, red ray,
      Warmed him with rosy feathers where he lay.

Far overhead streamed on the signal meteor,
  The Ariadne of the maps, who slowly
    Unwound the light and reeled the darkness up.
Love filled with fierce delight the humblest creature
  As heaven fills an eye, or as the Holy
    Infinitude the wafer and the cup.

Shepherds and kings and cowboys knelt around
  And marvelled that, while they could feel the
      power
    Whose rapture roars in God, yet God should
      moan:
And while His glory raised men off the ground
  (For Eve had brought such jewels in her dower)
    The tears of man should shine in God alone.

CHAD WALSH

Christmas in the Straw

In heaven it's Allemande Left and Promenade
And Swing That Corner Lady One And All.
This is the music that the fiddler played
When stars danced out of nothing at his call.

This is the dance the fiddler danced when Eve
Pranced to her feet from Adam's wounded side.
This is the song the fiddler sang at eve
Beside a cradle and his Jewish bride.

The angels sang the song the fiddler played.
The sheep and shepherds danced a Texas Star,
And wise men heard the music and obeyed;
The camels' feet kept rhythm with a star.

One and all, come this way.
Hear the fiddler sing and play.
Join your hands and form a ring,
Stamp your feet, dance and sing,
Hallelujah, now sashay!

On the Nativity of Christ

Rorate coeli desuper!
　Hevins, distil your balmy schouris!
For now is risen the bricht day-ster,
　Fro the rose Mary, flour of flouris:
　The cleir Sone, quhom no cloud devouris,
Surmounting Phebus in the Est,
　Is cumin of his hevinly touris:
　　Et nobis Puer natus est.

Archangellis, angellis, and dompnationis,
　Tronis, potestatis, and marteiris seir,
And all ye hevinly operationis,
　Ster, planeit, firmament, and spheir,
　Fire, erd, air, and water cleir,
To Him gife loving, most and lest,
　That come in to so meik maneir;
　　Et nobis Puer natus est.

Synnaris be glad, and penance do,
　And thank your Maker hairtfully;
For he that ye micht nocht come to

To **you** is cumin full humbly
Your soulis with his blood to buy
And loose you of the fiendis arrest—
And only of his own mercy;
Pro nobis Puer natus est.

All clergy do to him inclyne,
And bow unto that bairn benyng,
And do your observance divyne
To him that is of kingis King:
Encense his altar, read and sing
In holy kirk, with mind degest,
Him honouring attour all thing
Qui nobis Puer natus est.

Celestial foulis in the air,
Sing with your nottis upon hicht,
In firthis and in forrestis fair
Be myrthful now at all your mycht,
For passit is your dully nicht,
Aurora has the cloudis perst,
The Son is risen with glaidsum licht,
Et nobis Puer natus est.

Now spring up flouris fra the rute,
Revert you upward naturaly,
In honour of the blissit frute
That raiss up fro the rose Mary;
Lay out your levis lustily,

Fro deid take life now at the lest
In wirschip of that Prince worthy
Qui nobis Puer natus est.

Sing, hevin imperial, most of hicht!
Regions of air mak armony!
All fish in flud and fowl of flicht
Be mirthful and mak melody!
All *Gloria in excelsis* cry!
Heaven, erd, se, man, bird, and best—
He that is crownit abone the sky
Pro nobis Puer natus est!

A Cycle of Praise

The roads of our village amble
Through views of four seasons.
The eye loves and follows
The ritual year through occasions
That dazzle all seeing, humble
All knowing. Changes are heard:
Spring drums in the little hollows,
The to-and-fro borne bird
Of summer chirrs, the pageant
Autumn trumpets on the hills.
All sceneries lie urgent
On the heart. All are a praise
To Him whose laughter wills
Our glory-be of days.

Especially now do we feel
His sounding joy and His dare:
When sun-dials point winter
And daylights grow fainter;
When Advent hallows our streets

In a snowfall of prayers.
From windows our fire-trees
Wink azure devotions,
Because His birth bells peal
Alarums of love at our gates,
And we wake with His innocence
In us. The year ends here,
But we begin, in the air's dance
Of bright adorations.

W. H. AUDEN

FROM *For the Time Being*

NARRATOR

Well, so that is that. Now we must dismantle the
    tree,
Putting the decorations back into their cardboard
    boxes—
Some have got broken—and carrying them up to
    the attic.
The holly and the mistletoe must be taken down
    and burnt,
And the children got ready for school. There are
    enough
Left-overs to do, warmed-up, for the rest of the
    week—
Not that we have much appetite, having drunk
    such a lot,
Stayed up so late, attempted—quite unsuccessfully—
To love all of our relatives, and in general
Grossly overestimated our powers. Once again
As in previous years we have seen the actual Vision
    and failed

To do more than entertain it as an agreeable
Possibility, once again we have sent Him away,
Begging though to remain His disobedient servant,
The promising child who cannot keep His word for
   long.
The Christmas Feast is already a fading memory,
And already the mind begins to be vaguely aware
Of an unpleasant whiff of apprehension at the
   thought
Of Lent and Good Friday which cannot, after all,
   now
Be very far off. But, for the time being, here we
   all are,
Back in the moderate Aristotelian city
Of darning and the Eight-Fifteen, where Euclid's
   geometry
And Newton's mechanics would account for our
   experience,
And the kitchen table exists because I scrub it.
It seems to have shrunk during the holidays. The
   streets
Are much narrower than we remembered; we had
   forgotten
The office was as depressing as this. To those who
   have seen
The Child, however dimly, however incredulously,
The Time Being is, in a sense, the most trying time
   of all.
For the innocent children who whispered so ex-
   citedly

Outside the locked door where they knew the
     presents to be
Grew up when it opened. Now, recollecting that
     moment
We can repress the joy, but the guilt remains
     conscious;
Remembering the stable where for once in our lives
Everything became a You and nothing was an It.
And craving the sensation but ignoring the cause,
We look round for something, no matter what, to
     inhibit
Our self-reflection, and the obvious thing for that
     purpose
Would be some great suffering. So, once we have
     met the Son,
We are tempted ever after to pray to the Father;
"Lead us into temptation and evil for our sake."
They will come, all right, don't worry; probably
     in a form
That we do not expect, and certainly with a force
More dreadful than we can imagine. In the
     meantime
There are bills to be paid, machines to keep in
     repair,
Irregular verbs to learn, the Time Being to redeem
From insignificance. The happy morning is over,
The night of agony still to come; the time is noon:
When the Spirit must practise his scales of rejoicing
Without even a hostile audience, and the Soul
     endure

A silence that is neither for nor against her faith
That God's Will will be done, that, in spite of
    her prayers,
God will cheat no one, not even the world of its
    triumph.

Notes on the Poets

❂　　❂　　❂

W. H. AUDEN (1907–　　)
was the most influential British poet of the 1930s.
He came to America in 1939 and is now an American
citizen. The two poems used here are from
his Christmas oratorio, *For the Time Being*.

DANIEL BERRIGAN (1921–　　)
is a Roman Catholic priest. His first book of verse
won the coveted Lamont Poetry Award for 1957.

JOHN BETJEMAN (1906–　　)
is devoted to Victorian churches, old-fashioned
customs, and traditional verse forms. His *Collected
Poems* (1958) surprised the skeptical publishing
world by becoming a British best seller.

WILLIAM BLAKE (1757–1827)
was a visionary poet whose seemingly childlike
poems expressed an intensity of mystical experience. A skilled engraver, he frequently illustrated
his own verse.

ROY CAMPBELL (1901–1957)
born in South Africa, was by turns a bullfighter, a
soldier fighting for Franco, a fascist, and eventually
a convert to Roman Catholicism. His tempestuous
life ended in an automobile accident in Portugal.

PETER CHAMPKIN (1918–   )
was captured by the Germans at Dunkirk, and
eventually liberated by the Russians, finding his
way back to England via Odessa. The author of
four books of verse, and a highly original poet, this
is the first time his work has appeared in the United
States.

G. K. CHESTERTON (1874–1936)
a convert to Roman Catholicism, was one of the
most effective literary advocates of Christianity. His
poetry, little affected by modern stylistic trends,
has a rollicking verve.

SAMUEL TAYLOR COLERIDGE (1772–1834)
was one of the most gifted of the English Romantic
poets, as well as a literary critic whose influence is
still discernible in modern approaches to literature.

W. H. DAVIES (1870–1940)
was born in a public house in Monmouthshire, of
Welsh parents. A tramp during much of his life—
a train cut off a foot in Canada—he published his
first volume of verse at his own expense. Fortu-

nately he mailed a copy to Bernard Shaw, who recognized the uneven but haunting talent.

JOHN DONNE (1573–1631)
was equally famous as a poet and preacher in his own time. His work has had an extraordinary influence on twentieth-century verse.

WILLIAM DUNBAR (c.1460–c.1520)
was a Scottish Chaucerian. He served as a sort of poet laureate to both the Scottish and English courts, and his kind of poetry—with its strong interest in nature and human psychology—pointed toward Robert Burns.

LAWRENCE FERLINGHETTI (1919–   )
has been a central figure among the "San Francisco poets," as a poet himself and as a publisher. Many of his poems are written for oral presentation with jazz accompaniment.

ROBERT FROST (1874–1963)
was born in California, grew up in New England, and received his first poetic recognition while living in England. He became the unofficial poet laureate of America when he participated in President Kennedy's inauguration.

THOMAS HARDY (1840–1928)
was born near Dorchester, the son of a stonemason. By preference a poet, he devoted many years to

prose fiction, returning at last to verse when he could afford to. He is one of the few writers equally gifted in the two genres.

GEORGE HERBERT (1593–1633)
a country parson, is remembered for *The Temple,* a cycle of devotional poems. His tone is gentler, less paradoxical, less consciously intellectual than that of John Donne.

ROBERT HERRICK (1591–1674)
is one of a long line of Anglican priests who also have been important poets. The sacred and the secular mingle easily in his verse, which treats even the most serious subjects with a casual ease.

JEREMY INGALLS (1911–   )
is the author of several prose works, *The Galilean Way* and *The Epic Tradition,* but remains primarily a poet. Her major volumes of verse are a collection, *The Woman from the Island,* and a long narrative poem, *Tahl.* A native of Gloucester, Mass., she is now resident in Tucson, Ariz.

ROBINSON JEFFERS (1887–1962)
was the master of the long-cadenced line which he powerfully employed to depict a universe in which mankind is the alien intruder. The poem included in this book is more conventional in form, and gentler in tone, than most of his work.

JAMES JOYCE (1882–1941)
is best remembered for *Ulysses* and *Finnegans Wake*, in which he extended the scope of the novel beyond anything previously attempted. His poetry, much less known, is as simple as his prose is complex.

SY KAHN (1924–   )
has served as a Fulbright professor in Greece and is now associate professor of English at the University of the Pacific. His most recent book of poetry is *Triptych*. At present he is writing a study of Kenneth Fearing.

ARNOLD KENSETH (1915–   )
is pastor of the South Congregational Church in Amherst, and a member of the English faculty at the University of Massachusetts. His second book of verse, *The Holy Merriment*, established him as an outstanding religious poet.

HENRY WADSWORTH
LONGFELLOW (1807–1882)
author of *Evangeline* and *Hiawatha*, was one of the most widely read American poets of the nineteenth century, as well as a gifted translator of foreign poetry.

ROBERT LOWELL (1917–   )
is related to James Russell Lowell, Amy Lowell, and President Lowell of Harvard. Since the publi-

cation of *Lord Weary's Castle* (1946), which won
the Pulitzer prize, he has been recognized a major
figure among the newer American poets.

PHYLLIS MCGINLEY (1905–   )
is in private life Mrs. Charles Hayden, the mother
of two daughters. She has published numerous col-
lections of poetry and has an unusually wide
readership.

WILLIAM MCGONAGALL (1830–1902)
was born in Edinburgh of Irish parents. An ama-
teur actor as well as wandering rimester, his verse
deals with crowned heads, catastrophes, festivals,
and the scenes of everyday life.

VASSAR MILLER (1924–   )
was born in Houston, Texas, where she now resides.
Her earlier poetry is written mostly in strict forms,
but the later is somewhat freer. Religious subject
matter predominates, often treated with passionate
intensity.

HOWARD NEMEROV (1920–   )
teaches at Bennington College, and has at various
times been a lecturer at the Salzburg Seminar, and
Consultant in Poetry at the Library of Congress.

BINK NOLL (1927–   )
with degrees from Princeton, Johns Hopkins, and
the University of Colorado, is author of *The Center*

of the Circle. After teaching at Dartmouth and spending a year in Spain on a Fulbright scholarship, he joined the English faculty at Beloit College.

CHARLES OLSON (1910–   )
was one of the Black Mountain College group of poets. His theories on the composition of verse are exerting an increasing influence on many of the younger American poets.

JOHN FREDERICK NIMS (1913–   )
is professor of English at the University of Notre Dame. A gifted poet in his own right, he has also translated the poems of St. John of the Cross.

ROBERT PACK (1929–   )
is a coeditor of the well-known anthology *New Poets of England and America*, as well as being a widely published poet himself. He teaches at Middlebury College.

I. A. RICHARDS (1893–   )
born in England, is a university professor at Harvard. Famous for his work in literary criticism and semantics, he more recently has become known as a poet.

EDWIN ARLINGTON
ROBINSON (1869–1935)
was born in Head Tide, Maine, and grew up in

Gardiner, the "Tilbury Town" of his poetry. His understated and psychologically complex work is only now coming to be recognized at its full worth.

MAY SARTON (1912–   )
daughter of the historian of science George Sarton, was born in Belgium and grew up in Cambridge, Mass. A selected edition of her poetry, *Cloud, Stone, Sun, Vine*, was recently followed by her new novel, *Mrs. Stevens Hears the Mermaid Singing*.

WILLIAM SHAKESPEARE (1564–1616)
deals with Christmas in passing. The passage used here is part of a speech by Marcellus while discussing the ghost of Hamlet's father.

WINFIELD TOWNLEY SCOTT (1910–   )
was born in Haverhill, Mass. For many years he was literary editor of the *Providence Journal*. He now makes his home in Santa Fe.

CHRISTOPHER SMART (1722–1771)
was well known in London as a pamphleteer and satirist. He gradually went insane, one of his oddities being his habit of kneeling in heavy traffic in order to "pray without ceasing." He is remembered now for his long, uneven, but at times very beautiful work, *A Song of David*.